MASTERCLASS:

BLOW-JOBS

ALICE METCALFE

MASTERCLASS

THE *Erotic* Print Society
London 2003
First Reprint October 2005
Second Reprint January 2007

Alice Metcalfe would like to thank Jonathon Green and
Nicholas Campion

THE *Erotic* Print Society
EPS, 17 Harwood Road
LONDON SW6 4QP

Tel (UK only): 0800 026 25 24
Fax: +44 (0)20 7366330
Email: eros@eroticprints.org
Web: www.eroticprints.org

Printed and bound in Spain by Bookprint S.L. Barcelona
ISBN 1-898998-72-8

MASTERCLASS:

BLOW-JOBS

ALICE METCALFE

EPS

CONTENTS

Introduction   Page 6

Techniques   Page 16

Positions   Page 60

All in the Best Possible Taste   Page 76

Conclusion   Page 84

A Dictionary of Terms   Page 88

INTRODUCTION

How to read this book

Welcome to my blow-job masterclass. I hope you will find this book informative, helpful and, most of all, stimulating. First of all I want you to consider why you bought this book. Did you buy it as a couple? Is it a gift? Are you a generous woman hoping to spring a few surprise delights on her man? Whatever the reason, this book has something for the reluctant practitioner, the enthusiast, the connoisseur and the curious.

As you will see throughout this book, I don't prescribe one particular method of achieving the ultimate blow-job. It will pay to try out different things each time, not always in the same order, and you might find you come across the perfect formula. The best outcome for me will be if you discover that rather than one ideal blow-job, there is endless, exquisite variety! In the same way, to get optimum pleasure from your masterclass, read this book in whatever order comes naturally. Skip pages whenever you feel like it, but don't forget to refer to parts you may previously have neglected (a bit like the 'job itself!) and hopefully, this little resource will never be far from your bedside table.

What is it about a blow-job?

What is so special about fellatio? What is its relationship to 'normal' coitus? The weight of emphasis men sometimes place upon getting head as opposed to a fuck can be disconcerting for many women, especially as the act is perceived to be a little one-sided in the pleasure stakes. I hope that the sceptical out there will find, with the help of this book, that oral sex can be an integral part, the apotheosis even, of lovemaking.

The attraction of a blow job for many men is the psychological aspect as well as, perhaps even more than, the physical pleasure. I will elaborate on mind games later on in the chapter on techniques and positions, but there is room here to muse on the mental and emotional implications of sucking cock.

The novelty and rarity aspects of the act gives it a sort of wow factor — like the old joke 'Why's a blow job like lobster

thermidor? Because you don't get either at home'. This sort of gag reinforces the associations oral has not with wives, but with whores and mistresses and the idea (perpetuated by the men, if I'm not wrong) that giving blow jobs will keep your guy at home and stop him from straying. If head is only dished out for special occasions like birthdays and Christmas, it will be perceived as being done so somewhat begrudgingly or as a favour. That's not to say it has to be delivered on demand, every time; this is a dance of two partners. It will take concessions, compromises and consideration to feel your way as to how much head you want to partake in.

Some women are wary of giving head as they feel it is humiliating and submissive for the female to kneel in front of a man and suck his cock. There is some truth in the suspicion that it makes a chap feel powerful to see his chap being serviced thus. But please be understanding, for, as my lover once told me, 'When I was a young, wanking pre-teen, I never imagined I'd ever get a girl to look (and not laugh), never mind touch, my willy, least of all do me the pleasure of putting it between her lips.' Fellatio as validation of manhood cannot be underestimated, girls. Besides, he can't be totally in control when he puts the tenderest, most precious part of his person 'twixt your jaws — one false move and his love-tube is history! Ok, you can uncross your legs now, boys.

The blow-job is much prized amongst certain young women as a way of preserving virginity. Whereas at my school the idea that you might have done such a thing (I'm not sure we really knew what a blow-job was or that you weren't actually supposed to blow) was appalling, some cultures place such a high value on maidenhood that unmarried couples have more oral sex than anything else.

But despite the best attempts of religion and in some cases, the law, oral sex is a perfectly normal and natural act of love. There is a logic that labels fellatio (and buggery) unnatural as it does not contribute to the 'natural purpose' for humans to have sex — that of procreation. Many other ways in which we express desire also have no part in the begetting of children — kissing for example — and no-

one, other than the most perverted individual, would dare to suggest that that is unnatural.

No, the mouth is the place where we instinctively want to put things we love, and is used for a worldwide sign of affection — kissing. An attractive pout sells too, don't forget. You're not telling me that the crumbliest, flakiest milk chocolate in the world wasn't all the more alluring for being subject to camera close-ups whilst it was softly wedged between plump lips?

The tabloid-worthy sex scandal with its attendant salacious details has long been a national obsession. It is the peccadilloes and saucy titbits that fascinate and enthrall us, and can even mark someone's place in history. Pamela Anderson, Tommy Lee and the stolen video; Hugh Grant and one Miss Divine Brown on Sunset Blvd; a cigar-smoking US President, his plump-lipped intern (funny how that didn't count as 'sexual relations', isn't it?) and the incriminating photograph that led to her expulsion from polite society. All these stories date from the twentieth century,

and all but one from the last decade, yet
the blow-job still has power to fix itself in
the public consciousness.

TECHNIQUES

How to do it

This is the chapter with the stuff you really want to know about — how to do it. And how to do it better! In parts of this section I'll be addressing the fellater and at other times the fellatee, but it will be obvious who I'm talking to and when.

Let's start with the most important organ and its very special functions. The mouth, that is. The mush, along with the lips and tongue, can accomplish many useful things. This organ can lick, suck, bite, kiss, blow and chew. All of these actions may be employed during your oral lovemaking — admittedly some of the list a lot more gently and subtly than others. One other thing the mouth does can also be a wonderful boon in getting it right and that thing is — talk (or at least make noise). For both parties — giving and receiving — articulating your desires and feelings about what you do and don't like will ease the path to heaven-sent head. You might feel that it is unromantic to pause every so often to ask, 'Is this good for you?' Although you may have known your partner for a long time there is always something new to learn about them. I may

"I have a partner who is very keen on being fellated. Treating him to a superb episode of cock-sucking is a pleasure for me, too, as I love to give physical pleasure to my man! But a few months ago his enthusiasm for this treat started to wane. After some gentle probing, I elicited from him that while he found it sensually exciting, it had become a repetitive routine, and therefore slightly monotonous. So I realised that I would have to become a bit of a penis puppet-mistress and started to rub his dick in all sorts of different places on my body, in between sucks. It was more fun for me, too! A cock between your breasts, your thighs, pussylips or simply rubbed on your clit, can make it a lot more entertaining for the giver — your rewards, if you like, for a job well done!"

consider myself an expert on the subject, but in the course of researching this book, I quizzed my loved one about various techniques and even I found it difficult sometimes to keep a straight face out of embarrassment. Of course the natural place for asking questions is in the bedroom. 'Do you like this?' 'Could you do more of that' 'The kids are out, aren't they?' etc, but try having a discussion over a drink or the washing-up; a neutral situation can render different responses. Breaking off every 30 seconds for an update might be excessive but do make sure you both indicate when something is the source of pleasure or indeed pain. I know from experience that some of you former boarding-school boys out there have made an art form of the silent, expressionless climax. It must be all that after-lights-out action, with matron and masters lurking, waiting for a single incriminating peep out of their mastur-bating, adolescent charges. So loosen up! Speak out! Ask and you shall receive...

Right! Let's go on with the show – what happens when you get down there with the old chap? I'd like to start by saying that there is no fixed pattern for a really good blow-job. I have been told by my 'close friend' that variety and spontaneity will do the trick, thanks very much. You know those instructions for formal dancing with aerial views of what the feet should be doing, and a-one and a-two and a-three, cha, cha, cha? This is not like that. Yes, after a while you may find a sequence of events that works for you, and that will be a wonderful thing, but until then, try a mixture of moves and have fun doing it!

Bearing that in mind, there are, however, probably only one or two methods that will produce the erection itself and in turn the orgasm (if that is your goal – remember, though, to make an omelette you need to break a few eggs, but you don't have to make an omelette with 'em, do you?). The idea is that you both have an enjoyable learning experience in the meantime.

Getting there
It started with a kiss

My 'close friend and research assistant', who will remain nameless, thinks it very courteous and rather sweet to give his penis a gentle kiss (I think he really gets off on the reverence). But there's something to be said for encouraging an erection by just being enthusiastic. While you're down there it might be nice to do what I like to think of as a quick oral recce. Breathe warmly all

around the crotch area, kissing the insides of the thighs, kiss, lick and stroke his tummy and gently feel his testicles. If this is done with the lightest of touches, it can be extremely arousing. The effect is that of putting off the main meal with a series of delicate hors d'oeuvres if you will. A little gentle nibbling will drive the recipient wild with delicious frustration.

Opposite Page:
A Gentle Kiss
This Page and Following Page:
A Quick Oral Recce

Sucker!

If the penis is not in an erect state by this point, some more direct action is called for. The most efficient way to achieve a hard cock is simply to SUCK. I'm going to introduce a concept that may sound a little crude, but it is what a blow-job is all about: use the mouth to mimic the pussy. Take his

"I was fortunate enough to be blown by two girls at once. This sounds actually better than it is. If the girls know each other well, there might be some sort of empathy there and they would, I suppose, get their act together. These girls didn't know each other well and there was a sort of chaotic free-for-all that ended up with one of them taking on a much more manual role while the other sucked away. I didn't feel that I could stage-manage the whole thing because I didn't want to push my (already considerable) luck. There were better things ahead."

organ and draw it in and out of the mouth with the lips firmly round the shaft (mind the teeth!) using a series of long, deep strokes both slow and fast. Hey presto – a stiffy, I guarantee you. It is absolutely possible, and also commonplace, to complete the whole act in this way. It will probably give you an aching jaw before the curtain comes down. Although this book is going to put some smiles on some lucky faces, my prescription for trying out different moves and techniques

is intended to save some budding fellatrices from gagging and lockjaw. So for mutual pleasure, consider some of the following techniques.

Some magic tricks...

The lick of love

Ladies, if you're finding that you're getting tired after a few minutes of the 'sucker' technique and, jolly glad though you are to have a fine, erect specimen before you, are worried that you won't be able to carry on for much longer, this next trick will delight and heighten the senses. Place your hand between his abdomen and penis for a bit of leverage, pull the head of his penis towards you and locate the frenulum (this is the bit

Below and Following Page:
The Lick of Love

"My girlfriend has quite a small mouth and I (though I say it myself) have quite a thick cock. She finds it really jaw-achingly difficult to get much more than the top of the glans inside her mouth and I find it rather nerve-wracking when her teeth start to chomp down on the most sensitive part of my cock. So we've reached a sensible compromise. She puts some edible massage oil on her hands and starts off with a straightforward handjob. Then as soon as I'm hard and well into the whole thing she brings her mouth down on the tip of my dick. It's like being kissed by an angel!"

of tissue that joins the skin on the shaft to the heart-shaped head, or glans, of the penis.) The lick of love is the rapid flick of the tongue along this piece of tissue. This is also known as the butterfly flick, possibly because the gentle, yet distinct, strokes should be like the fluttering wings of that insect. It's a good way to give your jaw a rest, although it is demanding on the tongue, particularly the root of the tongue,

Bonding

A note to both parties — making eye contact at this point can prove a bonding exercise. The same goes for making your approval known through sounds — moans and slurps of pleasure. I'm assuming that you're not porn stars, so this has to some from the heart and should come with time — and mutual trust.

so you may need brief breaks at intervals (he won't notice because his cock will feel like a stick of dynamite!). The tongue should be firm and pointy — these are sharp little lizard licks — and execute as many quick flicks as you can. Don't worry if he doesn't respond after only a few, as this can involve a short build up. It is certainly worth trying out and persevering with. I have known it to have the 'No, stop! No, don't stop, for God's sake!' effect.

Just one Cornetto...

The psychological aspect of a woman going down cannot be underestimated and is discussed elsewhere in this book. My 'close friend', who, as you may have gathered, enjoyed assisting in the researching of this book, says that is the the visual aspect of getting head that accentuates the pleasure of the physical. It's not all about pumping

This Page and Following Pages:
Just One Cornetto

like a piston on his John Thomas or performing novelty acts worthy of a Taiwanese ladyboy. There are things you can do that don't require skill or practice — but what you will both need are trust and appreciation. When a man can see his own erection in his lady-love's fair hand it can be very gratifying. Ditto seeing her take long licks up and down his shaft, open-mouthed (hence the analogy with the famous ice-cream). It signifies enjoyment and relish and to an extent devotion, in the same way canines show love and gratitude. No, I'm not comparing you to a dog, but it is one way of indicating that this is done with love and not under duress as something you want to get out of the way as quickly as possible.

The sore thumb
This is something which at times I think I might have invented myself, although I doubt it very much. Lovers have reacted to this little trick with, 'What was that?' (in a good way, of course) and so I suspect it is overlooked in the blow-job repertoire. I call it the 'sore thumb', although it has nothing to do with the simile, 'sticking out like...'.

"Although I'm not a great one to swallow a man's cum, I do like the sensation of it jetting softly into my mouth. Sometimes, with a former partner, I would 'give him a taste of his own medicine' and 'snowball' it back into his mouth. We had a slightly S&M relationship, with both of us swapping roles. He always said that he didn't mind the taste of his cum as long as it was mixed with my saliva, or better still, my pussy juice! In my experience most men have to wank themselves off in order to come in fellatio, but a finger or a vibe (don't forget to lubricate them first) up the arse can work miracles in that department: then it's 'Look no hands!' and he comes like a fucking fire hose!"

Forgive the painful allusion but imagine you've hit your thumb with a hammer — the first thing you would do is jam it straight into your mouth and suck on it hard to provide a numbing relief from the pain (saliva has anaesthetic properties). The instinct to do so is healing and protective. During good head I will break off from the

suction-pump action and suck hard for a few seconds on a part of the penis (the glans is a good place for this) like one would a sore digit. It's like a quick, mini love-bite, drawing the blood even closer to the surface, causing a sexy tingling sensation.. Try concentrating particularly on the glans and around the frenulum if you want a

Firm Meat

Don't worry too much about sucking hard on a man's penis — unless he indicates otherwise, of course. Although the genitals of both sexes are delicate and sensitive, the male erection is quite firm meat and can take a thorough slurping.

Opposite Page:
The Sore Thumb

reaction — in this area a 'sore thumb' can be exquisitely too much to take. I love it!

The stuff of legend...

So, if you were to give head in this order — but I'm not saying that you have to, of course — you might be ready to take the whole penis back in your mouth. The next manoeuvre I'm going to discuss is almost the stuff of legend — yes, it's Deep Throat (DT). This is a bit of a controversial subject. It is mostly described as being difficult to do but something of a thrill both psychologically and physically. I have seen DT

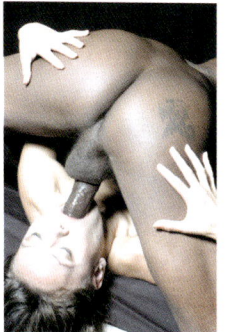
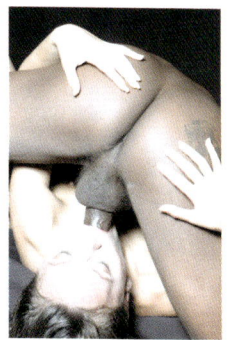

referred to in extremely negative terms in the course of my research, which surprised me a great deal. I can only imagine these accounts were coloured by contemporary gender politics. One article described Deep Throat as 'diabolically dangerous... more so than sword-swallowing' and 'only for psychopaths', another declared it 'non-existent, in fact technically impossible'. I know the last statement to be entirely untrue, it is not impossible, though it isn't by any means easy. As for the author of the other comments, whilst I respect her opinion... well, she's wrong.

DT isn't for everyone, but then again neither is oral sex full stop. But I'm a great believer in trying things at least once and it was that belief which led to the discovery of my own modest DT skills. Deep Throat isn't quite what the name suggests. If you are generously engaging your man in fellatio and want to try taking more in than usual, don't imagine that 'deep throat' means that his member will be massaging the bottom of your neck — not unless he is a phenomenally well-hung freak of nature. DT is the 'swallowing' of the penis. Many men are fascinated with the whole concept

of DT — particularly if they have never had it and/or have ever seen a copy of the famous Linda Lovelace film. Whilst not 'technically impossible', DT is quite hard to do, as it is not a natural thing to ask of your throat and overcoming the gag reflex takes time and effort. My deep throating came about by accident. During a rather tipsy and enthusiastic blow-job, the head of my lover's organ just sort of pushed through and I thought, 'Oh, so that's what it's like!' In my case I was lucky in that it just well, happened. I felt a tangible 'pop' as my man's penis forced down my epiglottis. It's the epiglottis that stops you from choking and prevents food and liquids from entering the lungs by cutting off the windpipe when you swallow. If you swallow a penis, the epiglottis moves in to do its natural function which means that breathing is restricted. Add to this the body's gagging reaction to a large foreign object headed towards the oesophagus, and, well, yes, DT is pretty damn difficult. I find that it can only be maintained for a few thrusts. The key is to relax and practice if it's something that you really want to give. The way to ease his pole down your throat is to take a tip from the sword-swallower

"When I was a student, I was regularly treated to a bj by my then girlfriend; one day she asked me if I would mind if she sucked a boiled sweet at the same time as sucking me off. Nothing ventured, nothing gained, I thought, and gave my unreserved approval. It was brilliant! The presence of another, hard but free-floating, 'agent' in her mouth was extremely novel and arousing. The sensations could be heightened, too, by using strong mints, which had a sort of 'cooling' effect when she came off the glans and blew, giving some sort of credibility to the famous term. She also pointed out that when I came inside her mouth she found it easier to swallow my cum, flavoured, as it was, by whatever she was sucking at the time. Beats a pierced tongue any day..."

and put your head back so that the O of your mouth is aligned, as opposed to at right angles, with your throat.

Faux Deep Throat

Determined to do Deep Throat? It's worth practicing on a similar object, a banana, for instance. You will become familiar with your boundaries and at which point your gag reflex kicks in etc. This is the start of overcoming them by pushing yourself a little bit further each time. Use this technique on the lucky penis that's getting it but remember, you are meant to be enjoying it, too! A sort of faux-Deep Throat can be achieved by sliding the penis deep into the cheek to give a sense of depth, The cheek is flexible, so having a cock push against it might be less of a struggle than one straining to get down your throat. It will most likely give any man a thrill to see the bulge of his penis in the side of your face, to be frank!

A note on good manners, here, gentlemen (and these rules are applicable to blow-jobs in general). You are only really going to get DT if you help out here. You both need to be in a comfortable position and, fellas, that means you need to maximise the chances of getting your cock down her throat by lying (sitting and standing positions are harder for DT) with your penis pointing down the sword-swallowing cavity she is making. The man who wants it deep but is in a position where the penis needs to be brought to the mouth at an angle with the assistance of the hands is not making things easy for himself or his cocksucker. As a fellow sexpert describes it, 'He's just going to be pounding away at the back of the throat. It's like trying to jam a pencil down an elbow pipe

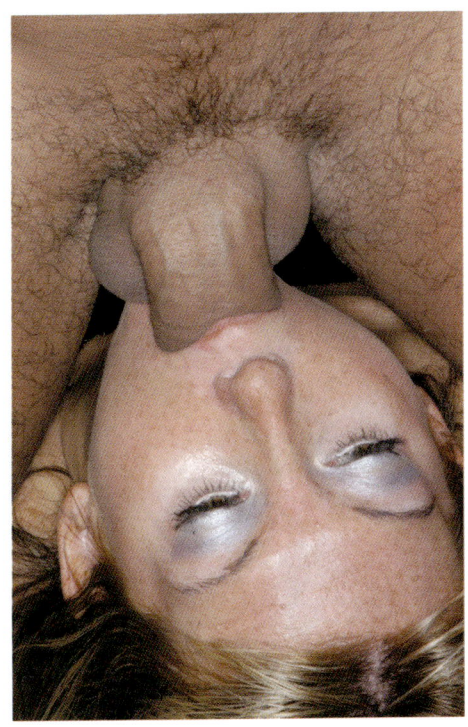

joint.' My other point about courteousness and oral pleasure is please DON'T push her head down. She's got her face in your crotch. You are getting head. It might result in a bit of DT. Don't push your luck, sonny. Pushing her head down on your penis is very bad form indeed. Unless grabbing your woman by the hair saying, 'Take it all,

bitch,' is something you mutually enjoy in an acknowledged sub-dom dynamic, don't do it! Hold her head, yes, stroke her hair, fine. But believe me, she really doesn't need a hand with getting your cock further into her gob. Plus, during or when attempting DT, pushing a woman's head could be potentially dangerous as well as bloody annoying.

But back to giving it deep-style. Potential DTers – this might take a lot of practice and some of you may never find it easy or even possible to do. It's not the end of the world, there are many other things you can be getting on with, which is the whole point of this book!

Don't!

All too often we find that we haven't enough time to devote to our partners and to lovemaking. Spare time is a precious commodity and few of us seem to have any to do things like pay the bills and repaint the skirting boards, let alone squander it on pleasures of the flesh! The great thing about blow jobs is that they're ideally suited to a quickie, although I know a man who really likes to make them last.

I once spent a whole day teasing my lover by starting a blow job and not finishing it, telling him he'd be in for a big treat later. Another way to guarantee him a heart-stopping orgasm (actually, if he has a dicky ticker, seriously, you might want to give this a miss) is to delay his ejaculation first, the build-up will be tantalising.

When you feel your man is approaching orgasm, continue to stimulate him a little, but gently. Then pinch his organ with your forefinger and thumb at the base of his penis. Think of it as literally as closing up his urethra disabling the process of ejaculation. He will not spurt as his body is telling him that it ain't gonna happen — though it is possible that he will still experience orgasm or sensations close to it, yet will not lose his erection.
When you find time to indulge yourselves, this little trick is a must!

Play ball
Q: Why do women rub their eyes first thing

"The man I'm with loves me talking dirty and generally 'vocalising' my desires and feelings while I blow him. As an actress, this comes quite easily to me. First of all I start talking about his cock and how it's getting harder and harder in my mouth and how I can't even take the whole of it's head inside my mouth, then I move on to admire his balls as I lick or jiggle them in their pouch, and so on. Ok, I'm well aware that it's corny as hell, but saying things like, 'God, I want your big, juicy cock to shoot all the thick creamy cum in your balls into my mouth and over my lips... my pussy's so wet, please do it now!' between sucks tends to have a very beneficial effect on the proceedings."

in the morning?   A: Because they don't have testicles. Chaps are very protective about their balls, and seem to be constantly adjusting them. As with all things it's different strokes for different folks, but a good blow-job can be enhanced by a few ball games. The most important thing to remember is go gently! This is a very sensitive part of his body and long fingernails and teeth are not good ball-bedfellows. Hold or stroke his scrotum tenderly during fellatio. Kiss him round that area, gently nibble at his inner thigh and lick his testicles. Take one or both of his balls into your mouth and gently suck (known as 'teabagging').

Cleanliness

I'd like to give this area a special mention. Lads, your balls can get a bit clammy being slung into briefs or boxers all day – give 'em a wash if you're expecting her to nuzzle them.

Humming

When you have a testicle or two in your mouth, try humming or making noise from your throat. The resulting vibrations will, if nothing else, make him smile! Or you could try a whole song; may I suggest 'Land of Hope and Glory'?

Kiss my...

Although they may not like to admit it on the grounds that it has some ridiculous associations with homosexuality, a man's arsehole is also an erogenous zone. A friend, Chris, once described how his Brazilian girlfriend gave him a blow-job and sensing his impending orgasm, 'stuck her finger right up me bum'. The consequence was a very intense orgasm for Chris and 'an ejaculation like a bloody geyser'. The anus is a mass of nerve-endings and sensitive to the touch. Try rubbing a lubricated finger gently around the area when giving head. The perineum, which is the skin between the penis and the arsehole, is similarly sensitive, in case any of you are squeamish about actual butt stuff.

And of course, what you can do with your hands you can do with your mouth, too. Licking the anus, or rimming, is not going to be everyone's idea of a fun thing to do and would be strongly advised against by some on health and hygiene grounds. As you're all grown-ups I'll let the decision rest with you. Make a judgement call on how comfortable you are with it, but I will say one thing — no-one ever died from kissing ass!

Above:
Rubbing a finger around his perineum
Following Pages:
Rimming

Bon Appétit!

There has always been a relationship between food and sex. The tastes, textures, smells and, of course, the activity itself, let's face it, can be an erotic experience. If you want to enjoy your man-meat meal all the more, it can be fun and rewarding to smear a little something on his cock and lick it off. Some foodstuffs are obviously more appropriate than others and sweet, rather than savoury, somehow feels the right way to go. But if your idea of very heaven is a ball-sack covered in Marmite, then far be it for me to stand between you and a good time!

While we're on the subject of these sensory titbits, bear in mind the temperature of the little extras you introduce into your blow-job. Some extremes (not so extreme that one of

Following Pages:
Food and Fellatio

you ends up in casualty) of hot and cold will stimulate different sensations. Try popping an ice-cube into your mouth as you suck him, alternating between hot and cold to really keep him guessing. Don't underestimate the tingling qualities of a good champagne either, or the delicious numbing feeling that you get from anything menthol. Suck on an extra, extra strong mint and then on his glans — it will give the same stinging sensation to his penis that it does to your mouth.

POSITIONS

I read in the *Kama Sutra* about pushing the tip of your tongue, having made it as hard and pointy as possible, into the guy's pee-hole opening at the tip of his cock. Different men react differently to this. Some love it, others hate it, but few seem indifferent! Sometimes I've done it just as the guy is coming – not easy with all the movement going on, but it's wild – like sitting on a geyser that's about to blow! I always find that the most fulfilling thing about fellatio is the moment of ejaculation – it's as if you've reached the end of your journey.

There is quite possibly an entire *Kama Sutra* of oral positions available and there isn't room here to go into the mechanics of all of them, so I'd like to run over the pros and cons of some of the basics.

On your knees...

A big part of the thrill of a blow-job for him can be looking down on you while you service him as he sits or stands. Is there a

This Page:
On Your Knees
Opposite Page:
A quick one in the office

man alive who, on seeing a woman on her knees, lapping away, worshipping at the great altar of love that is his cock, does not think, 'I should bloody well think so too'? Actually, I have met men for whom receiving head is no great shakes, but I've found them to be in the minority and I imagine that for the blow-

The On-Your-Knees-job

The On-Your-Knees-job is a great position for a quickie, especially if you are after some spontaneous sex somewhere unusual, for example a shop doorway or a nightclub fire escape (it, ahem, happens, believe me)

"Both my partner and I love food... and sex. We get up to some fairly crazy things in the kitchen and as we cook, drink and generally relax after work... well, one thing tends to lead to another. One evening we were fooling around before we had some friends around for a meal and we had made lots of different dips. I was starving and feeling quite horny. So I put some of each dip on a plate and started spreading them, one by one, on his dick. Sucking my guy's cock with a guacamole coating with alternate sips of cold white wine was pure heaven. So obviously I had to try the taramasalata, too. It was yummy. By the time our guests arrived, I'd 'tested' all of the dips and I wasn't feeling quite as hungry as before."

job fan, the dynamics of this position are a BIG thrill. It's also one of the things that some women object to about oral — that it is demeaning and subjugates the woman. I have no answer to this because it really depends on all sorts of things — beliefs,

Above:
Missionary with a Twist

generation, politics and how you feel about the light sub-dom associations of giving head.

Missionary with a twist

Again, this is a position that requires a lot of trust and cooperation from him as you could be vulnerable to choking. The woman lies beneath while he is on top using his arms (as if he were doing press-ups) to lever himself in and out of her mouth, literally 'face-fucking'. This too looks and feels like a dominant position for a man and

"Here's a tip for men who have problems persuading their 'virginal brides' to suck their cocks: if you're both at a stage of advanced foreplay, move up her body and rub the head of your cock against her nipples, one after the other, making sure that she has a good view of the act. Not only is the sensation nice but it's also like a much more gentle introduction to your rampant organ. Less frightening and rather more poignant than just waving it in front of their faces and saying 'Suck on this!' — or so I've been told! The urge to give the old chap a little peck on his tip is, apparently, overwhelming. Things will probably go smoothly, blow-job-wise, from there on in."

is not something to be abused. It is quite physically demanding on both parties and rarely is it kept up for the entire duration of the blow-job. It is, though, a good position for him to control thrust and speed. One variation on this position is hanging your head off the bed, which will allow for some deeper penetration. But, as ever, gents, mind your manners by ensuring that this is not uncomfortable for your good mistress and be prepared to stop if it becomes so.

Get on top

If you are unhappy about the feeling of female subservience that some of the positions convey, sitting astride his legs, or chest for that matter, while you give head puts the ball(s) in your court, so to speak. You control the thrust and the various different techniques and he's putty in your hands. You have his most prized possession between your lips and he's trusting you to look after it. This is a position in which you have all the power. Let him know this by tying up his hands, thereby relinquishing him of all control – which could lead to a long and sweetly agonising session. A blindfold will sharpen his remaining senses and a gag will stifle his cries of ecstasy, cutting off one avenue of release which in turn will make his eventual orgasm one of extreme intensity.

Opposite Page:
Get On Top
Following Pages:
69, man on top

"From the time she's knelt down on the carpet and started to give me head, it takes me about two or three minutes for me to come in my secretary's mouth — sometimes even less. It doesn't happen as often as I would like. But whenever my wife tries it, although it's a very pleasant prelude to full-blown intercourse, we both know that the days of my blowing my load in her mouth without vigorous manual assistance are over. I find it a little sad that 'familiarity breeds contempt' in this way. I blame my penis entirely. For some reason the excitement of an illicit sexual encounter behind my locked office door acts like the best aphrodisiac in the world on him. I can't for the life of me think why..."

Wine me, dine me, 69 me...

Ah, the 'Breakfast of Champions'. This, if you don't already know, is named after the shape that a top-and-tailed couple make who are engaging in mutual mouth-to-genital intercourse. It's good because a) you're getting and giving, and b) it's a

Fem-dom experiences

The On-Top could prove a real fem-dom experience if you start and stop then don't let him come at all. And aren't all the most passionate love affairs stories of thwarted desire and frustration?

great position for that most gratifying and intimate moments — a simultaneous orgasm. The latter is not a myth, but nor is it that easy to achieve, especially as there's a lot to concentrate on during a soixante-neuf. You'll have fun trying, though!

Above:
69. woman on top
Opposite Page:
Sensory Deprivation

ALL IN THE BEST POSSIBLE TASTE

There are tons of lubricants on the market with different properties — heat, cold, flavour, texture. Experimenting with different lubes will also be rewarding and is a must for fans of combining mouth, hand and between-breast-jobs.

So, you've got it licked now, I hope. But what happens at the end of a successful bout of love-pump licking? The big question when it comes to the BJ finale is 'to spit or to swallow?' It's a very personal thing and where for some people the answer is, 'God, no! No one does!' for others, there is no question that it's only polite to sup up. I'm of the latter camp, myself. I can't imagine what you're otherwise supposed to do with it— run eyes and cheeks bulging to the sink and go 'bleurgh!' depositing the contents down the plughole? Some of you may be nodding thinking, 'that's exactly what you do'. Fair enough, but there are kinder ways of disposing of unwanted come. A box of tissues close at hand is a good idea as you can pluck one out and discreetly spit it out — your man will be too wasted on endorphins to notice if you gargled and blew bubbles with it, frankly. If you don't want it in your mouth at all, you can combine the ejaculation with something visually and psychologically excited. Most

"For some reason, I always thought that I was alone in thinking that men's crotches smelled of mushrooms. Not that I minded, in fact, it's really rather a sexy, musky and pleasant odour; what's more is that nowadays when I open a packet of mushrooms from the supermarket I sniff them on purpose and get this great association with oral sex! The other day I was talking to two girlfriends and they absolutely agreed with me, although in their experience it was stronger in some men than others. But we all agreed it was bad news if you didn't like mushrooms..."

men give the game away as to when they are about to come — you probably know your own fella's giveaway signs — and he is likely to be thrilled if you allow him to bank he deposit over your breasts. Equally, allowing a man to ejaculate onto your face could be very blissful for him, I appreciate it may not be for you. Being ejaculated over the face and breasts might be a tall order if you have only just begun to contemplate having oral sex at all. Many women will

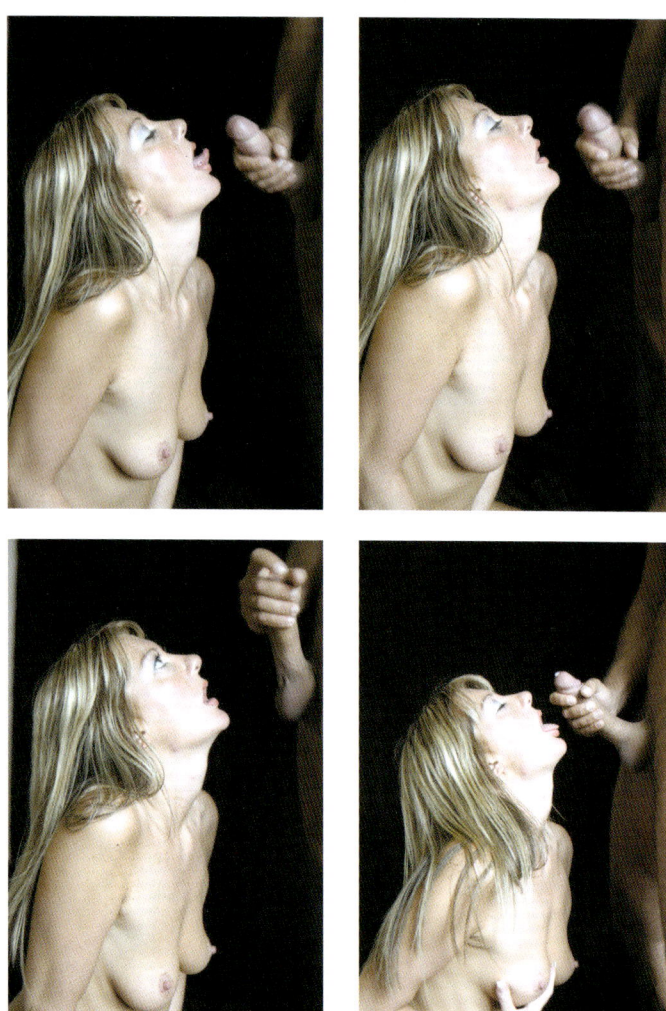

consider it degrading and a step too far, after all, it's not really something that we have the equivalent of giving, female ejaculation is a much less predictable phenomenon!

While we're on the subject, there is one myth I'd like blow (sorry) out of the water — if you're objecting to a mouthful of love juice on the grounds that you're a weight watcher, well calories schmalories, it's virtually fat-free, okay?

The viscosity and volume of semen will vary depending on how long it has been since he last ejaculated. The taste of a man's sperm varies from each individual, and although it can be subtly regulated by diet, it will still be very much his own personal bouquet! As for controlling the taste of his semen through what he eats — it's simply common sense; spicy foods and asparagus will produce a pungency that might prove unpalatable, whereas sweet things may in turn reduce the bitterness of his come. Possibly the best tip I have is to make sure he drinks plenty of water regularly as the hydration may produce a more bland ejaculate.

CONCLUSION

Go Forth and Blow!

I hope that you have enjoyed reading this masterclass, and that you have discovered many new things about yourself and your lover(s). It will take patience, understanding and, as I've said before, some talking to make oral sex and pleasurable and integral part of your lovemaking. As you have probably guessed, I am something of a blow-job devotee. I often wonder about other people's sex lives and am constantly astonished at what they will and won't do. Our attitudes towards sex are fashioned by so many different things — generation, upbringing and experiences. Also of course, everyone's physical responses are different; some have sensitive earlobes, others have erogenous elbows! My point is that I'm not really sure what 'normal' is, but I know what suits me. I hope that you find what's good for you and if that's a blow-job every Sunday or only once a year, then that's your normal. Just make sure it's a good 'un.

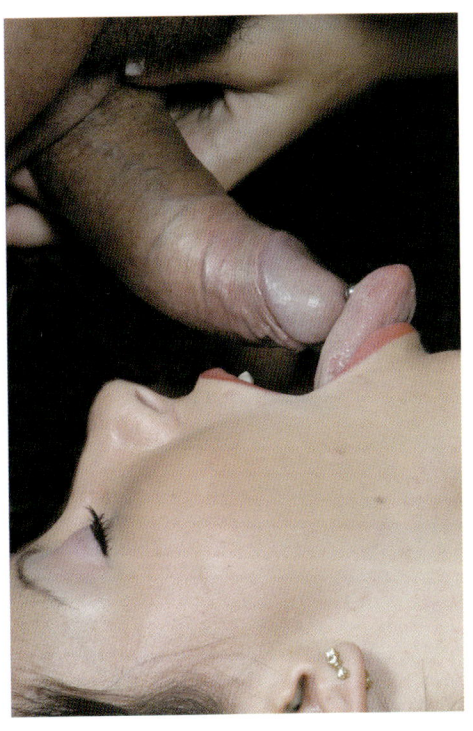

BLOW-JOBS:
A DICTIONARY OF TERMS

From Jonathon Green's *Dictionary of Slang*, published by Cassell

Oral Sex

army style [1960s+] (US gay)

flying sixty-six [20C] (rhy. sl. = French tricks)

French tricks [mid-19C-20C]

Frencher [20C]

head [1940s+]

header [1970s+] (US)

high Russian [1960s+] (plus simultaneous anal sex)

lip action [20C] (US)

lip dancing [20C] (US)

lip music [20C] (US)

lunch [1940s+]

moofty-poofty [1990s] (ext. of 'muff')

plating [1960s+] (rhy. sl. 'plates of meat' = 'eat')

skull job [1950s+]

tongue job [1960s+] (orig. US)

To Perform Oral Sex

bag [1950s+] (US Black)

chow down [1950s+] (US) (i.e. 'to eat')

eat [1920s+]

eat it [1910s+]

feed one's face [20C]

gamo/gammo [1910s+] (abbr. 'gamahuche')

get down [1930s] (US)

give a perm [1980s+] (US campus)

go below 14th street [1960s]

go down [1910s+] (US)

go down for the gravy [1950s+]

goop [1960s+] (US) (abbr. 'gobble the goop')

have lunch downtown [1920s+]

knock the dust off the old sombrero [20C] (US)

munch [1970s+]

orbit [1980s+] (one 'goes round' the genitals)

sit on someone's face [1960s+]

skull [1970s+] (orig. US Black) (play on 'head')

slob a knob [1940s+] (US)

swing low [1990s] (US Black teen)

Fellatio

Barry Johnson [1990s] (i.e. 'blow job')

basket job [1950s+]

blow job/b.j. [1940s+] (orig. US)

cherry blossom kiss [1990s]

cocksuck [1940s+] (orig. US)

cocksucking [20C] (orig. US)

deep throat [1970s+]

dicklick [1980s+] (US gay)

dicksucking [1970s+]

face [1960s+] (US)

face pussy [1980s+] (US gay)

face-fucking [1970s+]

fifty-fifty [1980s+]

French [late 19C+]

French culture [1960s+]

French head job [1940s+]

French love [20C]
French style [20C]
French way [20C]
gam/gamb [20C] (abbr. 'gamahuche')
gob job [1980s+] (US gay)
gobble [late 19C+]
gumjob [1980s+] (US)
gummer [1990s] (US)
half-and-half [1930s+]
hard mouthful [20C]
hat job [1950s+] (orig. US)
head job [1950s+] (orig. US)
hose job [1970s+] (US)
hum [1960s+] (US)
hum-job [1960s+] (US)
hummer [1960s+] (US)
knob-job [1960s+] (orig. US)
knobber [1980s+] (US campus)
kowtow chow [1980s+] (US gay) (lit. food eaten
while bowing the head)
larking [late 18C-19C]
larro [20C] (backsl. 'oral')
lid [1960s] (US)
lip service [1970s]
lip-lock [1970s+] (US)
meat whistle [1940s+] (US)
mouth fuck [mid-19C]
plate [1950s+] (rhy. sl. 'plates of meat' = 'eat')
pricknic [1980s+] (US gay)
s.m.s. [1990s] (US campus) (i.e. 'suckle my sac')
shiner/shiners [1990s] (i.e. the glistening spittle
on the penis)
show tunes [1960s+] (US gay)
sixty-eight [1970s+] ('you suck me and I'll owe
you one')
skull [1970s+] (orig. US Black)
skull fuck [1990s] (US)
skull-buggery [1990s]

slice of ham [20C] (rhy. sl. 'gam')
suck [1920s+]
sucking [1920s+] (orig. US)
white swallow [1990s]
zipper sex [1960s+] (US gay)

To Fellate

blow [1930s+]
blow off [1990s] (US)
blow someone's cookies [1930s+]
blow someone's glass [1970s+]
blow someone's/the pipe [1910s] (US)
blow the skin flute [20C]
brush someone's teeth [1980s+] (US gay)
bungle [1990s] (W.I.)
cap [1960s-70s] (US Black)
clean someone's/the pipe [20C] (US)
cop [1940s+] (US)
cop a bird [1940s] (US)
cop a/one's joint [1960s+] (US)
deep throat [1970s+]
do [1950s+] (US gay)
draw the blinds [1980s+] (US gay) (i.e. the
foreskin)
draw the curtains [1980s+] (US gay) (i.e. the
foreskin)
drink from the fountain of youth [1990s]
facial [1970s+] (US gay)
French [late 19C+]
gam/gamb [mid-19C+]
gamahuche [mid-19C+] (Greek gamos, a wedding
or Northumbrian dial. rouched,
wrinkled, puckered)
give cone [1980s] (US teen)
give head [1940s+] (orig. US)
hoover/hoover up [1970s+] (orig. US)
kiss [19C]

kiss the worm [1970s+]

kneel at the altar [1960s+] (US prison)

lay the lip [1970s+] (US)

lick log [1990s] (US)

line up on [1910s+]

make the blind see [1980s+] (US gay) (blind = uncircumcised)

mouth fuck [1970s+]

play the flute [20C] (US gay)

play the pink oboe [1990s]

play the skin flute [20C]

polish the knob [20C] (US)

polish the old German helmet [20C] (US)

prick-lick [1980s+] (US)

put some slobber on the knobber [20C] (US)

ride a blind piece [1960s]

smoke [20C]

smoke the baldy man [1990s]

smoke the big one [1990s]

smoke the blue-veined havana [1990s]

smoke the white owl [1990s]

spit out of the window [1930s+]

suck [1920s+] [1960s+]

suck off [1920s+]

swing [1970s+]

talk to the mike [1980s+] (US teen)

tongue lash [1930s+] (US gay)

whip some skull on [1970s+]

To 'Eat' the Penis

bite someone's crank [1960s+]

eat sausage [1980s+] (N.Z.)

eat someone's meat [1920s+]

gnaw the 'nana [1960s+]

gnaw the bone [1990s]

gob the knob [1990s] (US)

gobble [1970s+]

gobble hose [1980s+]

gobble the goo [1910s+] (orig. US)

gobble the gook [1910s+] (orig. US)

gobble the goop [1910s+] (orig. US)

gobble the goose [1910s+] (orig. US)

gum [1980s+] (US gay)

nosh [1950s+] [1960s+] (i.e. 'to eat')

plate [1950s+] (rhy. sl. 'plates of meat' = 'eat')

suck the sugar-stick [19C]

woof it [1980s+] (US gay) (i.e. wolf, to eat ravenously)

To Be Fellated

f.s. [1960s+] (i.e. 'face sit')

get face [1960s+] (orig. US)

get head/skull [1990s]

have one's hat nailed to the ceiling [1910s-30s] (US)

take it any way [1930s-40s]

A Fellator/Fellatrix

artiste [1980s+] (US gay)

barbecue [1930s-40s] (US Black) (i.e. 'a hot piece of meat')

blow job [1940s+] (orig. US)

bumper head [20C] (US)

chickenhead [1960s+] (US Black)

face artist [1970s+] (US Und.)

felicia [1980s+] (US gay) (mispron of 'fellatio')

French active [1950s+]

French by injection [1950s-60s]

French language expert [1950s+]

Frenchman [20C]

French passive [1950s+]

gap mouth [1990s] (US Black)

glutton for punishment [1970s+]

head-chick [1930s-40s] (US Black)
head hunter [1980s+] (US)
icing expert [1960s+] (icing = semen)
mouser [early 19C-1900s]
skull pussy [1980s+] (US gay)
smoker [1990s]
stool-pigeon [1980s+] (US gay) (play on stool = 'excrement')
Susan Saliva [1950s-70s] (camp gay)

sperm burper [1990s]
spigot [19C]
spunk-gullet [20C]
sucker [late 19C+]
suckster/suckstress [late 19C-1900s]
sword-swallower [late 19C+] (orig. Aus.)

As 'Eater' of the Penis

bone-gobbler [20C] (US)
choadsmoker [1960s+] [1980s+]
clarinet-player [1950s] (Aus.)
cocksmoker [1990s] (Ca)
cocksucker [late 19C+] (orig. US)
dicklicker [1960s+]
dicksucker [1970s+] (US)
dicky-licker [1930s+] (orig. US)
flute-player [1950s+] (US)
fluter [1970s+]
gobbledygoo/gobblegoo [1930s-40s] (US)
gobbler [1920s+] (US)
iron jaws [1980s+] (US gay)
knob-gobbler [1960s+]
lick-spigot [18C-19C]
meathound [1960s] (US Black)
mighty mouth [1950s-60s] (camp gay)
mouth-worker [1960s+]
muncher boy [1960s+] (US)
muzzler [1920s-50s] (muzzle = the mouth)
nob scoffer [1990s]
peter puffer [20C] (US)
peter-eater [1980s+] (US)
piccolo-player [1950s]
raw jaws [1980s+] (US gay)
scumsucker [1960s+] (orig. US)

Index

A

Anus, touching during a blow job, 52

B

Blow Jobs,
  Psychological Aspect of, 9
  Unnaturalness of, 12–14
'Breakfast of Champions', 71

C

Champagne, 59
Cleanliness, 52

D

Deep Throat, 36–47
Delaying his orgasm, 48
Divine Brown, 14

F

'Face-Fucking', 67
Faux Deep Throat, 44 Fem-Dom
Experiences, 74
Food, 56–59
Frenulum, 28

G

Get on Top, 69

H

Hugh Grant, 14
Humming, 52

J

Just One Cornetto, 30

K

Kama Sutra, 62, 62
Kissing, 14

L

Linda Lovelace, 42

M

Mints, 43, 59
Missionary with a Twist, 67

O

On Your Knees, 62, 65, 67
Oral Recce, 25

P

Pamela Anderson, 14
Perineum, 52
Play Ball, 48–52
Positions, 60–75

R

Rimming, 53

S

Semen,
  Flavour, 79, 82
  Disposal of, 78–79
  Viscocity, 82
  Volume, 82
Souixante-neuf, 71
Sucking, 24–26
S
unset Blvd, 14

T

Teabagging, 50
Teasing, 48
Techniques, 16–59
The Lick of Love, 27–30
Tommy Lee, 14

Some more titles available from the EPS:

MASTERCLASS: SEX TOYS   Dee McDonald

Another first for the EPS, this book takes a critical and informative look at the veritable toy cupboard of sex toys on sale at the moment and picks the best. Hardback, with beautiful colour photography. A hugely exciting publishing event.

£12.50

THE EPS KAMA SUTRA   Sir Richard Burton

What makes the EPS Kama Sutra stand out from the hundreds on the shelves today is that it is informed by a real couple, having real sex and being photographed in the process. This book examines the positions in a modern context and proves that this ancient manual still has a lot to teach us. Informative and arousing!

£19.95

SEXCITEMENT   Lynn Paula Russell

A beautifully illustrated, thrilling guide for couples who need to review and revitalise a tired sex life. An indispensable boost to any heterosexual partnership, which could take you to places in your sexual relationship that you never knew existed! Be warned, though: it examines very carefully what some would perceive as 'perversions'.

£19.95

SEX PLAY   Dr David Delvin and Lynn Paula Russell

This is the most definitive book on sexual foreplay ever written, with beautifully drawn illustrations by Lynn Paula Russell and an authoritative text by one of Britain's leading experts. Every couple's bedroom should have one: it's full of surprises for even the most sophisticated lovers, and remember — your sex life can only improve!

£19.95